Of Toxic Love And Growth

RB Gono

Published by RB Gono, 2021.

OF TOXIC LOVE AND GROWTH

First edition. January 28, 2021.

ISBN: 978-1393472339

Written by RB Gono.

Table of Contents

About the author

RB Gono is a Zimbawean-born poet. She is commonly known for her online poetry publications. RB has also written and released two novels and a few short stories online. She likes to describe herself as a curious mind and an old soul. She explores many themes in her writing, however her most prominent and favourite topics are shedding light on depression, religion, love and her perspective of the world to name a few.

OF TOXIC LOVE AND GROWTH

*Amidst the chaos of life and relationships, there
comes a point in life to reflect on the lessons we've
learnt and how we can move on from the relationships
that hurt us. This book speaks on the process of
allowing ourselves to heal, helping us reflect on those
circumstances and grow from our experiences*

Of Toxic Love & Growth

A Poetry Collection

RB Gono

OF TOXIC LOVE AND GROWTH

This is a love letter to the child in me who's hope was once lost. We searched high and low, fought a few foes until we found each other again. I love you dear child - I'll love you for life.

The journey of the creative

IT'S A CURSE
    To notice the way sunflowers sway with the moon
    Even though they don't like him
    I see heaven's smile in the sky sometimes
    And rename myself thankful
    For life is but a nightmare and a dream
    A nightmare that is my dream
    The breeze blows through my hair and I become weightless like a dandelion
    I'm flying through the minds of all those who've hurt before
    Looking through to my past life as a Spanish doctor
    Loving and true
    Hips wider than her guitar she dances every night to calm her relatives
    I'm flying into a future where skyscrapers are not high enough to reach my hopes
    Twinkling adventures in a city I've never been to
    Secret love affairs I have yet to encounter but have already felt and cried for
    Crying leads me into the ocean
    There I swim with the jellyfish
    Find peace among the reeds and reefs
    Smile and wake up alone in my bed
    A dream that was once a nightmare
    A nightmare that's now my dream

Another sacrifice for the winter

THERE IS NO GREATER love than this
    That one would lay down her life for her friend
    Let the Lord have Her fun
    And send me down the path of great sacrifice
    It is mine to discover
    Mine to wander
    A choice I made once and couldn't sleep with it
    Then I made it again and cried for 150 days
    I'll cry again- cry to death
    Cry that death loves me, more than I've ever loved myself
    Loves me enough to come early, to be there first
    To catch me
    There is no greater love than this
    That she would think of her neighbour just as herself
    Her majesty has spoken
    Let Her will be done
    That I would rather never love again than make a selfish decision
    So I'll spare the day an hour each
    To mourn the death of my winter
    Then wash it all off to go enjoy the sunrise
    Only to cry again at sunset

Real Love

I'VE KNOWN TRUE LOVE love
    Love love from my mother's hand
    Soft and unconditional
    I've known deep gut wrenching love love
    Love love that strikes the enemy in spirit
    She fights for me even in the realms that aren't physical
    My mother's love is pure
    Intentions Unselfish
    And for her love love
    I'd give my life
    But it's because of her love love
    That I stay alive

African

SUN KISSED
>My skin was rich from it
>I turned, letting the darkness that was always mine
>Fall
>Involuntarily behind me
>Confident I stared
>Expanding my sky
>So that who I am would not ever get in the way of where I would go
>Passionate it was
>Burning me with its lust
>Knowing that I would never shy away
>Sun-kissed
>My identity moved with it
>As it soaked me
>In love

Label me helpless

I DON'T CALL MY RAPIST a rapist
I call him by name
Speak of him like the shadow of a black cat scurrying across the wall, noticing me
Making chills run down my back
Because I'm scared
Him smiling then continuing on his journey into his keeper's arms
I do not call my experience rape
I call it relationship
Every I love you that I heard as let me fuck you
Every no that he heard as yes
Every panic attack I had in his presence that he didn't notice
Scolding me like: Why are you crying? Stop being so stressed, you're fine!"
I love how he never answered the phone when I couldn't breathe
How I was too great an expense
How he would say my name like it was a promise he was preparing to break every time he left but would never tell me
I don't call my rapist a rapist
I call him boyfriend, I call him ex, I call him a nice person
I call him teacher, friend and drunk stranger by The Rat
Because it's easier to stop breathing and smile than to get help
It's easier to say "I'm okay" in place of "This hurts, stop."
I don't call my rapist a rapist because then my name is Victim
My name is I'm sorry

OF TOXIC LOVE AND GROWTH

If I call him rapist my name is what were you even doing there?
And accuser
Who is this jerk?
Bitch.
When I just want to be called whole
I just want to be called love
I want to be star dust and sunshine
I want to be called free.

Cheaters

TELL ME HOW COULD YOU bear to call her and say you love her
    Then come into my shelter to give me a kiss
    How does your heart handle the caresses of my soft hand?
    The heat between my thighs
    Doesn't your heart remember her?
    About the fact that she has no body
    To hold, look at and look through
    She's not calling because she's bored – or suspicious
    But because love
    Because loneliness
    Because you promised you'd be there
    Always
    Yet here you are
    Holding the hand of a stranger
    Pulling me close like you'd like to stay here
    We know you won't
    Tell me how could you bear to call her and shout 'no other man!' whilst you've taken care of me?
    How do you think she sleeps at night knowing you're unfaithful but having no proof so she stays quiet?
    Loving you crazy- loving you insanely but never saying a word
    Because to say it out loud is to make it real
    And she'd rather have you than lose you to me

On friendship and heartbreak

TO ME FRIENDSHIP IS the plant I forget to water
    I know she needs sunlight so I take her outside
    Then forget her there, in a town where the scorching sun never sets
    Still she thrives, still she survives
    Turns into a tree that provides me with shade when I accidently lock
myself out
    When tears make my eyes so blurry I can't see the future
    She, is assuring
    Holds me tighter
    Friendship is the first girl whose heart I broke
    A toxic relationship
    And every time, without question she lets me abuse her again
    Believes my "I'll do better next time."
    Then watches me leave
    When she says goodbye it's packaged in love
    A war wife's farewell
    Always with a smile – always in pain

Someone Else

I CRY TEARS OF SORROW because Else can love me
>But Else can't be loved back
>Not by me
>Nor my willingness to let the winter go
>Not by surrender
>And not by pleasure
>I cry tears of sorrow because Else can love me
>But I might never love again
>Not because I don't want to
>But because the winter's soul owns mine
>And I try to run but all roads bring me back to being
>called 'mine'
>Because I am
>Because I can be

He has beautiful eyes

THE DEVIL HAS BEAUTIFUL eyes
    A chiselled face
    A confident boast
    He invites the broken
    Like myself
    Welcomes you with open arms
    Puts you in the back of an expensive vehicle
    Rides off into the sunset
    Only,
    The sun doesn't set here
    You realize it was never even there
    Those beautiful eyes turn red
    And burning needles, like chills run down your back
    Darkness.

First

MY SOUL HAS BEEN SEARCHING for yours from the time I
    learnt to comprehend emotion
    Writing love poems for a man I had never met
    Whispering prayers for a man who did not remember my name the
day we met
    My soul responds to the sound of your voice
    And eyes widen in your presence
    It excites me to think that I could look at you for the rest of my life
    My heart settles at the opportunity to love you,
    Forever
    In life and in death
    To have me searching for you in the next life
    To love you in a different city
    A different time
    A different way

Basic Human Decency

SOMETIMES I HAVE TO teach people to respect me
    The way they'd respect a street sign
    To listen to something that doesn't speak
    Something that never makes a sound but they always know what it's
not asking for
    I have to teach people how to say my name
    After they've used it to shame my parents
    And enslave my ancestors in superstition
    Used it to insult my Gods and take away my birth right
    How do I earn the right to be human?
    Hand me the instruction manual
    I am not asking for gold, or status or worth
    Simply your respect
    For you to recognize that I am deserving of life
    In whatever manner I choose to live it
    However, I choose to dress it
    Let my words manifest it
    Into my reality not yours
    Respect me
    Enough to say my name and my pronouns!
    Respect me
    Recognize that I am my race and my nationality!
    Respect me and know that when I step into the room I don't have to
make a noise for you to know how to act
    I am human, so treat me as such

RB GONO

I am human regardless of how I dress
I am human, no matter where I come from
I am human, doesn't matter what I like or who
I am human and so. Are. You.

On validation and neglect

I KEEP LOOKING FOR your name in things that involve mine
    As if you showing up validates my existence
    As if my voice is not heard until it's heard by you
    Until you challenge it
    As if,
    Until you tell me that I'm on the right path
    Nothing I do matters.
    I need to stop that.

The clouds

WHAT DO I THINK OF the clouds?
 I believe they're only a figment of my imagination
 They represent my heart
 Soft and tender, moved by the pressures that surround them
 Darkened by their desire which they live to absorb
 Fill themselves up until the burden is too heavy to lift
 And so they release
 Only to start over again
 They move from the Earth
 Lift themselves up to the heavens
 To get closer to God until their wicked ways defeat them
 Break down taking a part of them along
 I think the clouds are beautiful
 In the way that I am
 To bring hope during a drought
 Like joy to my depression
 And bring destruction to what's always pleasant
 Like anger to my loved ones

Interlude

Give love a chance
Wait for him
Give love some air
Let him live in you
Let him live for you

On love and Protection

I THOUGHT IT WAS LOVE

The way sleep eluded my father on nights where I was not sitting safely in his house

I thought,

That he was so obsessively protective

To think that no one deserved my time like he did

No one would make me smile like he could

None could love me more

I thought it was strict

To control the length of my skirts and the tightness of my pants

Declared I deserved freedom

Freedom to be free

Wild and free and pretty

I thought it was unfair

For him to talk about how he doesn't like red lipstick, or red nails and expensive perfume

How certain hairstyles were meant for 'grown women'

I realise now

That it was fear

The fear of holding a girl child in your hands

Promising to give your life to protect her

From those of your kind who do not respect your sacrifices

Who do not care for your wishes to raise a healthy, free child

Who see a child- without parental supervision – laughing freely in the sun

OF TOXIC LOVE AND GROWTH

The sun illuminating her teen thighs
Every skip causing her little butt cheeks to bounce
Fear.
That the moment he allows himself to rest
He puts trust in a malicious world that shows no mercy to women of
any age
The moment he turns around and allows me to exist on my own,
The vultures will pounce
Tear me up into itty bitty pieces
Strip me of the meaning of love replace it with desperation
My laughter into a warning sign for tears approaching
My life into a continuous death-wish

My name

MY NAME IS A PROMISE
   My name is an instruction
   Every time you call my name without doing the thing it says to do
   You're dishonouring my mother
   Who thought I was worthy of love
   You are spiting at my father who said I am to be worthy of trust
   My name my name is a promise
   My name my name is instruction
   Don't spit it at me without fulfilling the promise
   Don't shout it back without obeying the instruction.

Two Seats

TWO SEATS
   On the park bench
   Individual grins begun the journey to an unsatisfying joy
   Two seats
   In the taxi or at the back of the bus
   Whispering pink lies to one another
   Pink was pretty, pink was love
   Two seats
   At the back of the cinema
   Locking lips
   Lips where lies were created
   Sugar oozed out when we all entered the Promised Land
   Tasting the forbidden fruit
   Two seats
   In the church hall
   A dark monkey suit and tears in his eyes
   Three more steps to the door
   Just to run after her

For This Is

TO HAVE BEEN UNRELENTING in my pursuit
    was to see the sun rise in your eyes
        To chain myself to an idea and know that it was only a matter of time
        till I rename you mine
        For 'This Is'
        Is a declaration of love - a declaration of war
        Marking a territory across your treasure chest
        Signed This Is mine
        This Is worth
        This Is truth
        You are love
        Do you imagine
        That an angel would fly freely without her name?
        How then my heart, could you soar freely without mine
        Wrapped around your bicep
        Summoning you from your slumber
        Reeking of compassion and a gentle gaze of obsession
        Declaring war
        Singing This Is
        This is, love
        You are, you are loved.

Not of Corinthian love

IF LOVE IS PATIENT and you don't know how to wait
    For my body which you've not yet learned how to appreciate
    Then this is surely not love
    I've been taught that love is kind
    You, are not kind to me
    For kindness does not choose her working hours
    Kindness is always there
    Never a cause of despair
    Yours is conditional
    So then surely this is not love
    They say it does not envy, neither does it boast
    It is not proud
    You, my darling are a jealous king
    A prideful warrior, who's never gone to war for something noble like
my heart
    Your only battle is to keep it out of others nurturing hands
    Love would not use me to dishonour others
    After ignorantly dishonouring me
    Yes, I've let you fend for yourself in my crooked bones
    And forget me in the midst of your happiness
    You are easily angered
    By things that do not serve you a future
    Easily angered by my disrespect
    My disrespect in the form of me asking to be loved
    A little more Sire please

RB GONO

Save a little love for me
And when will you forgive me
For love keeps no record of wrongs
You tell me time and time again
That you cannot be with me because of how I broke us before
If your love cannot forgive me
Surely it is not love
So then I curl up under a waterless bridge
For I am a rebel without a cause – without a home
If what we share is not love
And I do not hate you
Then the ancient books forgot to write about cases like ours
Adam forgot to label this emotion
Perhaps it was the reason why God wanted to keep
us from the fruit
That you and I are the affair between the serpent
and Eve
A beautifully constructed lie
Neither love or hate
Just strong enough to ruin my name and have me addicted
But not enough to kill me until the Lord says yes

On parenthood and heartbreak

IMAGINE LOVING SOMEONE from the first heartbeat
    Before they know that to love you back is their only obligation
    See a vision of success in all possibilities
    Thinking one day whatever this child will touch will turn to gold
    Can you imagine knowing someone from their first breath?
    Knowing when they toss and turn in their sleep
    Transitioning into not knowing when they go to sleep at night
    And who they give their heart to
    I think parents know heartbreak like the colour of their skin after a
day at the beach
    Brittle, hard and sore to the touch
    But it heals- may leave scars but it heals
    I imagine that the creation of life is a task accepted by fools
    Knowing that one day your creation deserts you
    One day it stops trusting you – stops listening to your version of the
truth
    One day it leaves
    And goes off to be an individual
    Without supervision – without guidance
    Just a free and wild spirit
    With an anger that's misguided
    Oozing passion off the tips their hair and fingertips
    Ready to create for themselves
    I think parents know heartbreak like the dislocation of bones on
sports day

RB GONO

Painful and sensitive to the touch
Accompanied with laughter and the best memories

Poem #21

THE CURSE OF YOUTH is found in our ability to always
be so hasty.

Green Ophelia

I FANTASIZE ABOUT A future with you in my spare time
 An obsession I allow myself to entertain
 I see you coming home to me – your frustration eased by my smile
 My anxiety lifted by the sound of your roaring laughter
 I close my eyes and remember the way your hands feel
 When they are tracing my flabby arms
 Your lips on my forehead
 I like to dance to the memory of your heartbeat in the shower
 And practice all the times I will say I love you
 I love you
 I love you and perhaps hear it back
 I love you
 To be young and in love
 Is to remember the way the waves feel in December
 Rejuvenating, refreshing but oh so dangerous
 Because you haven't yet learned how to swim
 Yet here you are
 Splashing about in the water, laughing your lungs out
 Screaming I love you
 I love you
 I love you
 Simply hoping you'll hear it back and sometimes you do
 An echo bounces off the shore to form an I love you too

Recovery

FACING ONE'S DEMONS is a terrifying exercise

I spent most of my religious life being silent from fear of asking how to fight them

Demons are not to be mentioned in a religious household

Yet I knew how to avoid possession more than I knew how to pronounce my own name

I thought possession would feel a little like drunkenness

To be aware but out of touch

To not know how to break free

That facing my demons would be to look at myself in the mirror and hate what I saw

Have worthless strapped to my neck until it drove me mad

Instead,

The effort to ensure that I never got possessed is what choked me at night

I would do my model best to choose the right friends

Listen to the right type of music: "It's always in the music that the plant those subliminal messages baby"

Didn't drink or scream

Anger is a sign of possession

Didn't laugh too loud or cry – Discontentment is a sign of possession

Facing my demons felt a lot like bungee jumping

Deciding that I was done with controlling every molecule of oxygen that went up my nostrils, I allowed my body to breathe

That now in this moment I would let go

RB GONO

I stepped off the ledge, not sure if that was solid ground or water
beneath me
Whatever it was, it was dark and I was terrified
And just when I thought it would consume me
My body jerked upwards and I hung there in the midpoint
Swinging – free, hopeful
And happy I hadn't died.

Interlude 2

Yes, I've been attracted to broken people
And they loved the whole in me
Perhaps because all my pieces fit perfectly
in their broken
And that's why they wouldn't let go
Except they couldn't get my whole off
So they attached themselves to me instead
And we became one
But now I'm heavy
I'm heavy and I'm sore
Thinking life would be easier lived broken and light
Than whole and burdened

No more!

WHEN I WAS THE ONLY one here my name was the same as the one on my birth certificate

God given to my mother through her sweating pores and screaming lungs right onto your tongue

A promise you didn't want to acknowledge

When I was the only one here my call was a dreaded event

An obligation

Every hello met with 'you can hang up now, we've been speaking for too long'

Clamping my tongue as if to say speak no more

Your words are unnecessary

Your feelings though by my inspiration don't belong to me

But,

The day she came back my name changed and I was now called love and bestie

Waking up to a sunlit day and a vibrating 'hey sexy'

A pitiful but excited 'aren't you glad we're here again

Why are you upset?'

How come you can only love me when I'm a third party?

How come you return to me only when it's supposed to be wrong

Supposed to be secret, sinful, a Saturday autumn wind

To your favourite girl's scorching breath

I am

Not yours-to keep

Why am I upset?

OF TOXIC LOVE AND GROWTH

At the fact that I am perfect but just not perfect for you
Love you, don't stay though
By 'don't stay though', you mean love you
But from a distance
And only when you say so
Love you when you call me
Not a moment before then
And never call you – you will not answer
Don't I dare seek another
I belong to you but you are free as birth
Free as a prisoner fresh out of jail,
Eager to taste everything from the years he's missed
By 'don't stay though'
You mean to call me sweetheart
Say you're here to receive me
Throat open, teeth shining like at the feast of a vampire
Why am I upset?
I am your prey
Glazed over and hypnotized
Offering you my neck
So you can suck me empty and give it to her?
No more!

Notes from the mistress

HE LAYS ON TOP OF THE sheets

Like he is setting a boundary that he doesn't want to cross

But I watch his arms betray him as he pats for me to get closer to him in his sleep

He doesn't know of the way his fingertips reach for mine then grab my hands stroking them gently while he sleeps

He says my name like he's spiting it out but the taste won't leave

So he keeps spitting

Every so often he confuses it with love and hopes I don't notice

Stumbles over phrases he is not supposed to allocate to me

So he breathes and swallows – looks over to check if I was listening

Nods and hopes I don't notice

He sits across the room to create distance- like he didn't drive here by his own will

But I know of the way his eyes search my face when I'm not looking

Sometimes

When I lift my head his eyes say something he won't let slip out of his mouth

Since it stenches of betrayal

He is changing the way I see warm hugs when it's cold

Hand holding that comforts the soul

Since she lies on her bed at home

Wondering why it's always so quiet when she calls

So he leaves and I let him

Only he comes back and accepts disloyal as his name

OF TOXIC LOVE AND GROWTH

He will leave again
And I will let him until my own heart finds a home and I find
meaning in the word love again

Death is a funny thing

HE TURNS TO ME, TAPS me on my lower back
    Says he fears –
    Fears what?
    The parting of clouds on a cold morning?
    The breaking of hearts at sunset?
    No, my last breath, my lover fears my last breath
    His hand is more gentle than I remember
    He's strong and reassuring like the goodbye between a wave and the
shore
    Always concerned, always returning and repeating
    Says he fears
    But what does he fear?
    My death
    My lover fears my death

Recharge

AND WHEN YOU GET TIRED of giving a love that never returns
    Remember it's alright to take a break to love you
    When you've emptied yourself out
    To those who swear you matter "enough"
    Just not enough to be there when you need them the most
    Remember it's alright to be there for yourself
    And don't be afraid to go back
    Because to love is to suffer
    We've suffered for many things before
    And of all our battles this is the most honourable
    So cover your wounds to stop the bleeding
    Broken bones mend themselves eventually
    To love is to give
    But when you've given your all
    Remember to recollect and recharge

My Poem

MY POEM,
    Though a gathering of words on Colonizer Lane
    Is an accurate representation of the African in me
    A storyteller, tattletale for all the warriors crying in pain
    For a future they deserve but never asked for
    My poem, though a heartbreaker's psalm
    Is God's goodbye kiss
    On a forehead longing for thoughts that calm
    The mind into remembering that ignorance is bliss
    My poem is a peaceful existence
    Explaining how there is no gnashing of teeth to my joy
    No struggle to the obsession my skin has for my flesh
    A flesh that's clinging to my bones, a-hoy!
    We're boarding a ship called Hope
    Hoping to be seen as one in union,
    My poem summons Happiness from her sleep
    Calls her Beauty and Love and sometimes misnames her Sorrow
    Tells her she is ours to keep
    My poem-
    Is a constellation waiting to be created
    To be studied
    A rainy day waking up to the intoxicating smell of coffee
    My poem asks a few questions – its breath baited
    Questions like what is your name, who sent you here?
    And would you like to love me?

Aloe

I TOOK AN ALOE AND put him in my heart
    I gave him love, light and nourishment
    So much love, light and nourishment
    Too much
    Love, light and nourishment

Let me be your mirror

IF I LET THE WORDS hold on to my tongue
And refuse to let go
Let my mouth stay shut
Nothing will ever be heard from me
No screeching sounds of my desire
For a love I stumbled upon once- grabbed
Held on for dear life- ran and never looked back
To this day I'm still running
Eyes closed drenching myself in joyous oblivion
Running fast
Pounding the ground with my feet
Hoping that the sound they make sings to your shattered spirit
Your possessive spirit – your selfish spirit – your loving spirit
Running in hope that when I arrive you'll see your reflection in my sweat
Feel the heat emanating from the heart I never had before I met you
See how you taught me to love freely – unconditionally – Forgivingly – possessive
Marking a territory that can never be occupied by anyone that isn't God themselves
Even God themselves hasn't learnt how to make their presence that significant
A master class
Dripping with potential for all the empires to be build
All the hearts to be broken and heads to be rolling

OF TOXIC LOVE AND GROWTH

A king.
Mine.

Growth

PERHAPS GROWTH IS NOT the moment you learn to stop crying
   Perhaps growth is reaching the point where you understand that this situation makes you cry
   And that is okay
   I've been praying that I learn to stop crying every day since I was in 4th grade
   10 years later and every week is laced in some wave of sadness
   I cannot tell you where it came from
   I don't know if it'll ever leave
   All I know is that sometimes it changes its name
   Gets a new ID – so that sometimes I call it treasure
   But it feels all the same
   My pillow stains all the same
   My weekly ritual of crying myself to sleep continues
   Perhaps growth isn't me going to bed with a smile on my face
   Perhaps it's simply accepting that today I'm sad
   But trusting that the sun still rises in the morning
   And should I wish, I can rise with it
   If I don't it's okay it'll return to fetch me the next
   day and the day after that
   Until I am ready to follow it

Sweater weather

I KNOW A GIRL WHO LOVES me more than the colour red
Passionate is her desire
For my arm that yearns to pull her closer at night
She, lives a thousand kilometres away from me
But meets me every night in her dreams
Whispers my name before I disappear and she wakes up
I know a girl
A smart- ass that's wild and free
She has a grounded spirit
An old cultured soul
When she misses me she puts on my sweater
Lets it hang on her body
She pulls the sleeves passed her wrists and breathes in the scent I left
her
Lets it soak her tears before she falls asleep
To meet me where she left me.

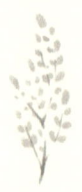

Declaration

THE WIND WHISTLES AND the swings outside my door
Squeak to join in the song
I hear the leaves rattle my praises
And my guides are calling my name
Singing this is the last time
This is the last time my heart will get disrespected
Not seen for it's worth
This is the last time
The last time I have to hit my head to remind myself that stupid people are not worth my time
That my love is rich and satisfying enough
Not to be advertised or petitioned
This is the last time
The last time my eyes swell up from tears of yet another stolen love
Another lonely night
Another heart on my table that I am not 'down' for
I won't compromise again
I won't hurt for mankind again
Won't bleed for love again
That was the last time
And now
I am whole wanted and worthy
Forever whole, wanted and worthy
Sing my song angels
Sing my song

OF TOXIC LOVE AND GROWTH

I am full of love and unbroken melodies
A tranced fire dancer raging in my heart space
Screaming whole wanted and worthy
Whole, wanted and worthy.

Beloved

I DESIRE TO KNOW WHAT it's like to be loved the first time
And have them stay forever
The way my mother loves – to be hurt by what hurts me
The way my father loves – to hurt what hurts me
I desire to know what it's like to meet a stranger that I deem lovable
for life
And have them see the same potential in me-
For life
I desire to know what it's like to be loved by someone who doesn't
constantly try to run away from loving me
Who refuses to believe that just because my name is Beloved that
means I get loved enough
They will say, "Here, here's some more
Some more, some more for you. I brought all this love here for you.

What sunshine feels like

I IMAGINE THAT MY SMILE to Heaven is an event worth celebrating

Like the parting of clouds after a heart startling storm

A resonance of my favourite song on high volume wearing headphones

Feeling my heart dance to the beat

I think the only reason smiling too long hurts

Is to remind us that even those things that are good for us hurt us sometimes – leave lifelong marks so as to mark their territory

Like the sun to my naked skin

A collection of heated kisses to the petals that surround my face

It's not shocking that happiness is a vacation destination

I love to visit repeatedly

An island where my lover's laughter is the song birds sing in the morning

Her kiss, the sunlight pushing through my curtains

This is not my voice

I CAN'T RUN FROM MY shame
 The shame I feel when I rise in a room full of light faces
 And they stare at me with pride
 For this is a voice they can relate to
 Pity the face is too dark
 The culture is too deep
 I can't run from my shame
 The shame I feel when I rise in a room full of dark faces
 And they stare at me confused
 Because they fail to locate the white girl whose voice booms through the room
 Pity the black girl who stands before them is not as brave
 Her culture is too shallow
 How do we forget?
 That human beings are creatures of influence
 How when you stressed to me how imperative it was that I learn English it made it easy to forget my mother tongue
 What did you expect?
 When you filled our schools with the European curriculum
 We began feeling like our ancestors' ways were foolishness
 So we changed the way we dressed, the way we prayed and what we sang about
 Humans are creatures of influence
 When you let the TV raise us we grew up thinking that to be American was the only way to be

OF TOXIC LOVE AND GROWTH

God bless America and no place else, right?
So they did
How could we not want to be just like the favoured ones of God?
Still I – cannot run from my shame
At how eloquently I speak
At how cultured I am
How relatable my struggle is
At how un-African my struggle is
I cannot run from my shame
At how foreign I feel in my own body
In my own continent, in my own world
To speak so passionately about things I'm told I'm not supposed to speak about
Okay...
Then whose voice is this?

On love and affection

PERHAPS
The best thing I ever did for myself
Was to recognise love in its many forms
From its many sources
So not to obsess over knowing a single well where I could quench my thirst
But instead be overwhelmed by the showers of compassion and affection
That dampen me at every turn

Affirmations

I DESERVE LOVE BECAUSE I love
    I am love
    I am whole, well and worthy
    Whole and worthy
    I thank myself for taking care of my body
    And giving me nourishment
    I am grateful for the time to connect with God daily
    And speak to them the way the angels do
    And they help me maintain
    My state of being
    Ensuring success in my endeavours
    I deserve love because I love
    I am love
    I am whole, well and worthy
    Whole and worthy.

Happily, ever after

IN THE END I'VE DECIDED that I am the star of this movie
    Therefore, I will always win
    No matter how many plot twists twist my heart strings out of tune
    I will always rise
    Find a tree branch to hold on to and get myself up onto the cliff
again
    I am- without the shadow of a doubt
    The damsel in distress and the hero in tight pants
    In the Camaro riding into the sunset
    Riding, riding
    Becoming a shadow against the light
    Riding, riding saying good morning to the night

Books By This Author

Little Girl Blue

Excerpts from Little Girl Blue
sad poem
I thought Solely to myself- (Yet not by myself)
That if I said more words that sounded a little more cheery
I might begin feeling that way
If my conduct was a little more friendly
Perhaps I would stop liking being alone
Alone not lonely- (I was always alone)
As I said these things I saw that you became a little hopeful
(I heard that sigh)
"Maybe she will marry before the night enraptures both of us"
So you started plotting that joyful
(Though slightly less to me)
Event
Without my consent
But I had promised that I wasn't going to shout
Never again would I scream—
(out loud)
Of the pressure I feel when you talk about how another's Child
In mine arms will make you proud
Not my way with words that unite a nation
(even if it is only for 60 seconds)
I promised that I would be pleasantly passive
Passionately peaceful

OF TOXIC LOVE AND GROWTH

To not speak of the things that make people frown
Rather say words like "how whimsical": when it's not
And "you're beautiful": when she's not
(not tonight anyway)
I apologize for that time when you hand me the mic
And I stay silent,
Screaming *happy songs damn it, sing happy songs!*
But this poet's soul reeks of perishable emotions
I have yet to clean out
Until then, with the stroke of the same pen
Here's another sad poem
(smiles)

The bilayer of existing There are silent cries
No tears, no noise, no heavy breaths
Yet inside your head you're screaming
Because everything that can cause pain does
Every reason to live life is a curse
So you end it
But the prayers of a past life
Bring you back- each time
A mercy you once praised suddenly you won't allow it to bring you
joy
Because pain is all you know
It's the cradle from where you won't leave
It is only when you see this
That you realize what you've become
Then the tears well up and drown your vision

OF TOXIC LOVE AND GROWTH

"Because"
"Because"
We don't start a sentence with because
But you did
Placed it in front of a gamble of other words
I did not hear
But understood
Since all they were doing was cutting through my heart strings
Burning through my arteries
Into the soul I never owned
"I love you."
We don't start a relationship with I love you
But you did
Placed them after paragraphs I didn't want to read
But I remember every word
Since they tapped into my well-hidden insecurities
And turned my dump yard into a garage sale
I realize now that words are what you have on me
They are my weakness
So possibly...probably
You will always win
Killing me over and over again with nothing but words
Every time you plunge another word in me: I die... And then I
resurrect
With tears accompanying a convincing smile
And an 'I'm sorry I took so long to make up my mind' I really
shouldn't live without you

About Falling in love

Opium sable rest tonight
If you think of her would you run to me
Into this vine that suffers blight
Ensure, please ensure that my soul makes it into the blue sea
My veins are made of anger
My blood has turned to ice
In my dreams you're willing to bag her
But in the real world the blue girl is nothing but nice
Opium sable kiss me to numbness
I'm stupid enough to jab you into my bloodstream once more
For a smile in the night is still a form of happiness
And denying myself of you has my heart declaring war
Ensure, please ensure that my blood never returns to red again
Ensure, please ensure that at the passing of the prayer you say amen
I can't say it for you since you know the oath my soul is meant to take
It's my time to die for you so ensure,
Please ensure the bed of thorns is made

Bed peace

Perhaps a little chaos is good for us
Like an unmade bed, it provides comfort and warmth
But only when a person is in it
If I allow you to be my chaos, would you let me in?
Maybe you're a lover of perfection
Yet you claim to love me—Now
It is time for the realization that like spring occurring in April
You cannot have perfection and I at the same time
Unless,
We conquer my world and change it
Making spring time in April a known phrase
And I become perfect
But love don't you see
Spring in April is not as perfect as it seems
As the chaos in me reigns like an African king:
With authority and envy
Arrogance and perseverance
The beauty in war
Is found at the frontlines of our bed peace
When I find your side made because you've never been in it
And mine falling off into the ocean of the dirty socks I wore when I
was attempting to run from you

The comfort of home

Freedom is coming home from a gruesome day and being embraced by kisses radiating with the pureness of sober affection

Freedom is not having to stifle a laugh

Being unashamed to cry

And it exists only in the place where I rest and retire my feet

Soaring far away from the sores the world inflicts on me

Freedom is my mother's smile

And her honesty

Which is never requested by my tongue

But perhaps a gait, or a vision I pay no attention to

It is a father who understands,

And finds peace in never forsaking his and his own

Loving endlessly and overwhelmingly to my annoyance

Freedom is comfort, freedom is home

About Him

Eyes are open— you're alive
"Thank Him for another day"
Open your eyes: my eyes are open— "give thanks"
Gratitude...gratitude?
For what am I grateful?
That he gave *us* black skin that you can't love
A green world that we can't share
Gratitude...
Oh Lord, our heavenly father
Here we are giving thanks
For this *gift*
Gift? This life is a gift?
Oh see how his sons take after him...
Angels and demons, this place is full of angels and demons
I can't tell which is which
So I must protect myself...why don't you protect me...father
Angels and demons
Life and death
You would gift me a world full of that
This is my gift
A world full of murderers, thieves, anxiety and anger
All this war, hatred, and so much hunger
This is my gift?
Oh! ...thank you.

Don't miss out!

Visit the website below and you can sign up to receive emails whenever RB Gono publishes a new book. There's no charge and no obligation.

https://books2read.com/r/B-A-TODL-LMTLB

BOOKS 2 READ

Connecting independent readers to independent writers.